Practical
Quick & Easy

p

This is a Parragon Publishing Book
This edition published in 2005

Parragon Publishing
Queen Street House
4 Queen Street
Bath BA1 1HE, UK

ISBN: 1-40542-312-9

Printed in China

NOTE

Cup measurements in this book are for American cups.
This book also uses imperial and metric measurements. Follow the same units
of measurement throughout; do not mix imperial and metric.
All spoon measurements are level: teaspoons are assumed to be 5 ml, and
tablespoons are assumed to be 15 ml. Unless otherwise stated,
milk is assumed to be whole milk, eggs and individual vegetables such as potatoes
are medium, and pepper is freshly ground black pepper.

The nutritional information provided for each recipe is per serving or per person.
Optional ingredients, variations, or serving suggestions have
not been included in the calculations. The times given for each recipe are an approximate
guide only because the preparation times may differ according to the techniques used by
different people and the cooking times may vary as a result of the type of oven used.

Recipes using raw or very lightly cooked eggs should be
avoided by infants, the elderly, pregnant women, convalescents,
and anyone suffering from an illness.

Contents

Introduction...4

Avocado & Lime Soup 6

Spicy Zucchini Soup...7

Avgolemono..8

Green Bean Salad with Feta...............................9

Baked Goat Cheese Salad 10

Mexican Salad...11

Chicken & Papaya Salad...................................12

Authentic Guacamole.......................................13

Aïoli 14

Tapenade 15

Chorizo & Garbanzo Tapas 16

Red Shrimp Curry 17

Fish with Black Bean Sauce 18

Herrings with Hot Pesto...................................19

Mediterranean Monkfish..................................20

Gingered Monkfish...21

Spicy Tomato Chicken......................................22

Chicken & Corn Stir-Fry...................................23

Skewered Chicken Spirals 24

Pork Stir-Fry with Vegetables..........................25

Stir-Fried Pork with Pasta................................26

Pork Balls with Mint Sauce..............................27

Vegetable Frittata..28

Introduction

This book is designed to appeal to anyone who wants a wholesome but quick and easy diet, and includes many recipes suitable for vegetarians and vegans. Its main aim is to show people that, with a little forethought, it is possible to spend very little time in the kitchen while still enjoying appetizing food. The recipes collected together come from all over the world and make full use of the exciting range of foods now available in local stores and supermarkets. The more exotic dishes on offer are balanced by some traditional recipes, which are sure to become firm family favorites. If you want fast food for everyday meals, or you are short on time and want to prepare a tasty dinner party treat, there is something for everybody in this book.

Pantry essentials

To save time in the kitchen, try to store staple foodstuffs such as rice, pasta, spices, and herbs, so that you can easily turn your hand to any number of these recipes.

Flour: you will need to keep a selection of flour. Self-rising, all-purpose, and whole-wheat are the most useful. You may also like to keep some rice flour and cornstarch for thickening sauces and to add to cakes, cookies, and desserts. Buckwheat, garbanzo, and soy flours can also be bought. These are useful for combining with other flours to add different flavors and a variety of textures.

Grains and rice: a good variety of grains is essential. For rice, choose from long-grain, basmati, Italian risotto, short-grain, and wild rice. Look out for fragrant Thai rice,

jasmine rice, and combinations of different varieties to add color and texture to your dishes. When choosing your rice, remember that brown rice is a better source of vitamin B1 and fiber.

Other grains add variety to the diet. Try to include some barley, millet, bulgur wheat, polenta, oats, semolina, sago, and tapioca in your stock.

Pasta: this is very popular nowadays, and there are many types and shapes available. Keep a good selection, such as basic lasagna sheets, tagliatelle, fettuccine (flat ribbons), and spaghetti. For a change, sample some of the many fresh pastas now available. Better still, make your own: hand-rolling pasta can be very satisfying, and you can buy a special machine for rolling the dough and cutting certain shapes.

Beans: these are a valuable source of protein, vitamins, and minerals. Stock up on soy beans, navy beans, red kidney beans, cannellini beans, garbanzo beans, lentils, field peas, and lima beans. Buy dried beans for soaking and cooking yourself, or canned varieties for speed and convenience.

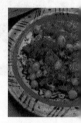

Herbs: a good selection of herbs is important for adding variety to your cooking. Fresh herbs are preferable to dried, but it is essential to have dried ones in stock as a useful back-up. You should store dried basil, thyme, bay leaves, oregano, rosemary, mixed herbs, and bouquet garni in your pantry.

Chiles: these come both fresh and dried and in many colors. The heat varies so use with caution. The seeds are hottest and are usually discarded. Chili powder should also be used sparingly. Check whether the powder is pure chili or a chili seasoning or blend, which should be milder.

Nuts and seeds: as well as adding protein, vitamins, and useful fats to the diet, nuts and seeds add important flavor and texture to vegetarian meals. Make sure that you keep a good supply of nuts, such as

hazelnuts, pine nuts, and walnuts. Coconut is useful too.

For your seed collection, have sesame, sunflower, pumpkin, and poppy seeds at hand. Pumpkin seeds in particular are a good source of zinc.

Dried fruits: currants, raisins, golden raisins, dates, apples, apricots, figs, pears, peaches, prunes, papayas, mangoes, figs, bananas, and pineapples can all be purchased dried and can be used in lots of different recipes. When buying dried fruits, look for untreated varieties: for example, buy figs that have not been rolled in sugar, and choose unsulphured apricots, if possible. These are often available from health-food stores.

Oils and fats: oils are useful for adding subtle flavorings to foods, so it is a good idea to have a selection in your pantry. Use a light olive oil for cooking and extra-virgin olive oil for salad dressings. Use sunflower oil as a good general-purpose oil. Sesame oil is marvelous in stir-fries; hazelnut and walnut oils are superb in salad dressings. Oils and fats add flavor to foods, and contain the important fat-soluble vitamins A, D, E, and K. Remember, all fats and oils are high in calories, and that oils are higher in calories than butter or margarine.

Vinegars: choose three or four vinegars—red or white wine, apple, light malt, tarragon, sherry, or balsamic vinegar, to name just a few. Each will add its own character to your recipes.

Mustard: mustards are made from black, brown, or white mustard seeds, which are ground and mixed with spices. Meaux mustard is made from mixed mustard seeds and has a grainy texture with a warm taste. Dijon mustard, made from husked and ground mustard seeds, has a sharp flavor. Its versatility in salads and with grills makes it ideal for the vegetarian. German mustard is mild and is best used in Scandinavian and German dishes.

Bottled sauces: soy sauce is widely used in Eastern cooking and is made from fermented yellow soy beans mixed with wheat, salt, yeast, and sugar. Light soy sauce tends to be somewhat salty, whereas dark soy sauce tends to be sweeter. Teriyaki sauce gives an authentic Japanese flavor to stir-fries. Black bean and yellow bean sauces add an instant authentic Chinese flavor to stir-fries.

Spices: your basic stock of spices should include fresh gingerroot and garlic, chili powder, turmeric, paprika, cloves, cardamom, black pepper, ground coriander, and ground cumin. The powdered spices will keep very well in airtight containers, while the fresh gingerroot and garlic will keep for 7-10 days in the refrigerator. Other useful items, to be acquired as your repertoire increases, are cumin seeds (black as well as white), onion seeds, mustard seeds, cloves, cinnamon, dried red chilies, fenugreek, flavored ghee, and garam masala (a mixture of spices that can either be bought ready-made or made at home in quantity for use whenever required).

You can use spices whole, ground, roasted, or mixed with yogurt to marinate meat and poultry. One spice can alter the flavor of a dish and a combination of several can produce different colors and textures. The quantities of spices shown in the recipes are merely a guide. Increase or decrease them as you wish, especially in the cases of salt and chili powder, which are a matter of taste.

Some recipes require roasted spices: you can use a heavy, ideally cast-iron, skillet for this. No water or oil is needed: the spices are simply dry-roasted whole while the pan is shaken to stop them from burning on the bottom.

Remember that long cooking over a lowish heat will improve the taste of the food because it lets the spices become absorbed. This is why reheating dishes the following day is no problem for most Indian food.

KEY	
Simplicity level 1-3 (1 easiest, 3 slightly harder)	
Preparation time	
Cooking time	

Avocado & Lime Soup

A delightfully simple soup with a blend of typical Thai flavors, which needs no cooking and can be served at any time of day.

NUTRITIONAL INFORMATION

Calories ....188 Sugars 2g
Protein ....3g Fat 18g
Carbohydrate ....4g Saturates 5g

15 mins | 0 mins

SERVES 4

INGREDIENTS

2 ripe avocados

1 small mild onion, chopped

1 garlic clove, crushed

2 tbsp chopped fresh cilantro

1 tbsp chopped fresh mint

2 tbsp lime juice

3 cups vegetable bouillon

1 tbsp rice vinegar

1 tbsp light soy sauce

salt and pepper

GARNISH

2 tbsp sour cream or crème fraîche

1 tbsp finely chopped fresh cilantro

2 tsp lime juice

finely shredded lime rind

1 Halve and pit the avocados and scoop out the flesh. Place in a blender or food processor with the onion, garlic, cilantro, mint, lime juice, and about half the vegetable bouillon, and process until completely smooth.

2 Transfer to a bowl. Add the remaining bouillon, rice vinegar, and soy sauce and process again to mix well. Taste and season, if necessary, with salt and pepper or with a little extra lime juice if required. Cover and refrigerate, until needed.

3 To make the lime and cilantro cream garnish, combine the sour cream, cilantro, and lime juice in a bowl. Ladle the soup into chilled bowls, spoon the lime and cilantro cream into them, and sprinkle with the lime rind.

COOK'S TIP

The top surface of the soup may darken slightly if the soup is stored for longer than about an hour, but don't worry—just give it a quick stir before serving. If you plan to keep the soup for several hours, lay a piece of plastic wrap over the surface to seal it from the air.

Spicy Zucchini Soup

Mild red chili powder and pan-browned garlic give flavor to this simple vegetable soup. Quick to make, it's ideal for a light lunch.

NUTRITIONAL INFORMATION

Calories	98	Sugars	.........1g
Protein	.........2g	Fat	...........7g
Carbohydrate	....8g	Saturates	.......1g

5 mins   20 mins

SERVES 4

INGREDIENTS

2 tbsp vegetable oil

4 garlic cloves, thinly sliced

1–2 tbsp mild red chili powder

¼–½ tsp ground cumin

6⅓ cups chicken, vegetable, or beef bouillon

2 zucchini, cut into bite-size chunks

4 tbsp long-grain rice

salt and pepper

sprigs of fresh oregano, to garnish

lime wedges, to serve (optional)

1 Heat the oil in a heavy-bottomed pan, add the garlic, and cook, stirring frequently, for about 2 minutes, until softened and just beginning to change color. Stir in the chili powder and cumin and cook over medium-low heat, stirring constantly, for a minute.

2 Stir in the bouillon, zucchini, and rice, then cook over medium-high heat for about 15 minutes, until the zucchini are just tender and the rice is cooked through. Season the soup with salt and pepper to taste.

3 Ladle into warmed soup bowls, garnish with oregano, and serve with lime wedges if using.

VARIATION

Instead of rice, use rice-shaped pasta, such as *orzo* or *semone de melone*, or very thin pasta known as *fideo*. Use yellow summer squash instead of zucchini and add cooked pinto beans in place of the rice. Diced tomatoes also make a tasty addition.

Avgolemono

The hallmarks of this traditional Greek lemon and egg soup are its fresh flavor and lightness. Serve it with olive bread or fresh rolls.

NUTRITIONAL INFORMATION

Calories	138	Sugars	.........1g
Protein	.........8g	Fat	...........6g
Carbohydrate	...15g	Saturates	.......1g

🍮 🍮 🍮

🍲 10 mins   🕐 12 mins

SERVES 4-6

INGREDIENTS

5 cups chicken bouillon

3½ oz/100 g dried orzo, or other small pasta shapes

2 large eggs

4 tbsp lemon juice

salt and pepper

fresh flatleaf parsley, finely chopped, to garnish

olive bread or fresh rolls, to serve

1 Pour the bouillon into a flameproof casserole or heavy-bottomed pan and bring to a boil. Sprinkle in the orzo, return to a boil, and cook for 8–10 minutes, until the pasta is tender but still firm to the bite.

2 Whisk the eggs in a bowl for at least 30 seconds. Add the lemon juice and continue whisking for another 30 seconds.

3 Lower the heat under the pan of bouillon and orzo, until the bouillon is not boiling.

4 Very gradually add 4–5 tablespoons of the hot (not boiling) bouillon to the lemon and egg mixture, whisking constantly. Gradually add another 1 cup of the bouillon, whisking to prevent the eggs from curdling.

5 Gradually pour the lemon and egg mixture into the pan, whisking, until the soup thickens slightly. Do not let it boil. Season to taste with salt and pepper.

6 Spoon the soup into warmed soup bowls and sprinkle with chopped flatleaf parsley. Serve immediately with olive bread or fresh rolls.

VARIATION

To make a more substantial soup, add 10½ oz/300 g finely chopped cooked, skinless chicken meat. This version uses orzo, a small pasta shape that looks like barley grains, but you can substitute long-grain rice.

Green Bean Salad with Feta

This fresh-tasting salad is flavored with fresh cilantro, an herb that resembles flatleaf parsley in appearance, but tastes quite different.

🕙 10 mins ⏱ 5 mins

SERVES 4

I N G R E D I E N T S

12 oz/350 g green beans, trimmed

1 red onion, chopped

3–4 tbsp chopped fresh cilantro

2 radishes, thinly sliced

¾ cup crumbled feta cheese

1 tsp chopped fresh oregano or
½ tsp dried oregano

2 tbsp red wine vinegar or fruit vinegar

5 tbsp extra-virgin olive oil

3 ripe tomatoes, cut into wedges

pepper

1 Bring about 2 inches/5 cm water to a boil in the bottom of a steamer or in a medium pan. Add the green beans to the top of the steamer or place them in a metal colander set over the pan of water. Cover and steam for about 5 minutes, until just tender.

2 Transfer the beans to a bowl and add the onion, cilantro, radishes, and crumbled feta cheese.

3 Sprinkle the oregano over the salad, then grind pepper over to taste. Whisk the vinegar and olive oil together and then pour over the salad. Toss gently to mix well.

4 Transfer to a serving platter, surround with the tomato wedges, and serve at once or chill until ready to serve.

VARIATION

This recipe is delicious made with *nopales*, or edible cactus leaves, which are available in cans or jars in specialty stores. Drain, then slice, and use instead of the green beans, missing out step 1. Replace the feta with 1–2 chopped hard-cooked eggs.

Baked Goat Cheese Salad

Scrumptious hot goat cheese and herb croûtes are served with a tossed leafy salad to make an excellent light snack, capturing Provençal flavors.

NUTRITIONAL INFORMATION		
Calories 509	Sugars 3g	
Protein 18g	Fat 33g	
Carbohydrate ...35g	Saturates 10g	

🥗 10 mins   🕐 10 mins

SERVES 4

INGREDIENTS

9 oz/250 g mixed salad greens, such as arugula, mâche, and endive

12 slices French bread, plus extra to serve

extra-virgin olive oil, for brushing

12 thin slices of Provençal goat cheese, such as Picodon

fresh herbs, such as rosemary, thyme, or oregano, finely chopped

DRESSING

6 tbsp extra-virgin olive oil

3 tbsp red wine vinegar

½ tsp sugar

½ tsp Dijon mustard

salt and pepper

1 To prepare the salad, rinse the leaves under cold water and pat dry with a dish towel. Wrap in paper towels and put in a plastic bag. Seal tightly and store in the refrigerator, until required.

2 To make the dressing, place all the ingredients in a screw-top jar and shake until well blended. Season with salt and pepper to taste and shake again. Set aside while preparing the croûtes.

3 Under a preheated broiler, toast the slices of French bread on both sides, until they are crisp. Brush a little olive oil on one side of each slice while they are still hot, so the oil is absorbed.

4 Place the croûtes on a cookie sheet and top each with a slice of cheese. Sprinkle the herbs over the cheese and drizzle with olive oil. Bake in a preheated oven, 350°F/180°C, for 5 minutes.

5 While the croûtes are in the oven, place the salad greens in a bowl. Shake the dressing again, pour it over the salad greens and toss together. Divide the salad between 4 plates.

6 Transfer the hot croûtes to the salad greens. Serve immediately with extra slices of French bread.

Mexican Salad

This is a colorful salad with a Mexican theme, using beans, tomatoes, and avocado. The chili dressing adds a little kick.

NUTRITIONAL INFORMATION

Calories 307	Sugars 7g
Protein 5g	Fat 26g
Carbohydrate . . .13g	Saturates 5g

10–15 mins   0 mins

SERVES 4

I N G R E D I E N T S

lollo rosso lettuce

2 ripe avocados

2 tsp lemon juice

4 medium tomatoes

1 onion

¾ cup canned mixed beans, drained

D R E S S I N G

4 tbsp olive oil

dash of chili oil

2 tbsp garlic wine vinegar

pinch of superfine sugar

pinch of chili powder

1 tbsp chopped fresh parsley

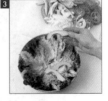

1 Line a large serving bowl with the lettuce leaves.

2 Using a sharp knife, cut the avocados in half and remove the pits. Thinly slice the flesh and immediately sprinkle with the lemon juice.

3 Thinly slice the tomatoes and onion and push the onion out into rings. Arrange the avocados, tomatoes, and onion around the salad bowl, leaving a space in the center.

4 Spoon the beans into the center of the salad and whisk the dressing ingredients together. Pour the dressing over the salad and serve.

COOK'S TIP

The lemon juice is sprinkled onto the avocados to prevent discoloration when in contact with the air. For this reason, the salad should be prepared, assembled, and served quickly.

Chicken & Papaya Salad

Try this recipe with a selection of different tropical fruits for an equally tasty and refreshing salad.

NUTRITIONAL INFORMATION

Calories 408	Sugars 8g	
Protein 30g	Fat 28g	
Carbohydrate ...10g	Saturates 5g	

5 mins   15 mins

SERVES 4

INGREDIENTS

4 skinless, boneless chicken breasts

1 red chile, seeded and chopped

2 tbsp red wine vinegar

5 tbsp olive oil

1 papaya, peeled

1 avocado, peeled

2 cups alfalfa sprouts

2 cups bean sprouts

salt and pepper

TO GARNISH

diced red bell pepper

diced cucumber

1 Poach the chicken breasts in boiling water for about 15 minutes, or until cooked through.

2 Remove the chicken with a slotted spoon and set aside to cool.

3 To make the dressing, combine the chile, red wine vinegar, and olive oil, season well with salt and pepper, and set aside.

4 Place the chicken breasts on a cutting board. Using a very sharp knife, cut the chicken across the grain into thin diagonal slices. Set aside.

5 Slice the papaya and avocado to the same thickness as the chicken.

6 Arrange the slices of papaya and avocado, together with the chicken, in an alternating pattern on four serving plates.

7 Arrange the alfalfa sprouts and bean sprouts on the serving plates and garnish with the diced red bell pepper and cucumber. Serve the salad with the dressing.

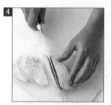

VARIATION

Try this recipe with peaches or nectarines instead of sliced papaya.

Authentic Guacamole

Guacamole is at its best when freshly made, with enough texture to really taste the avocado. Serve it with vegetable sticks or tortilla chips.

NUTRITIONAL INFORMATION

Calories	212	Sugars	. . . . .1g
Protein	. . . . .2g	Fat	. . . . .21g
Carbohydrate	. . . .3g	Saturates	. . . . . . .4g

15 mins   0 mins

SERVES 4

INGREDIENTS

1 ripe tomato

2 limes

2–3 ripe, small to medium avocados, or 1–2 large ones

¼–½ onion, finely chopped

pinch of ground cumin

pinch of mild chili powder

½–1 fresh green chile, such as jalapeño or serrano, seeded and finely chopped

1 tbsp finely chopped fresh cilantro leaves, plus extra to garnish

salt (optional)

tortilla chips, to serve (optional)

1 Place the tomatoes in a heatproof bowl, pour boiling water over to cover, and let stand for 30 seconds. Drain and plunge into cold water. Peel off the skins. Cut the tomatoes in half, seed, and chop the flesh.

2 Squeeze the juice from the limes into a small bowl. Cut 1 avocado in half around the pit. Twist the 2 halves apart in opposite directions, then remove the pit with a knife. Carefully peel off the skin, dice the flesh, and toss in the bowl of lime juice to prevent the flesh from discoloring. Repeat with the remaining avocados. Mash the avocado flesh fairly coarsely with a fork.

3 Add the onion, tomato, cumin, chili powder, fresh chile, and cilantro to the avocados. If using as a dip for tortilla chips, do not add salt. If using as a dip for vegetable sticks, add salt to taste.

4 To serve the guacamole, transfer it to a serving dish, garnish with finely chopped fresh cilantro, and serve with tortilla chips if using.

COOK'S TIP

Try spooning guacamole into soups, especially chicken or seafood, or spreading it into sandwiches on thick crusty rolls. Spoon guacamole over refried beans and melted cheese, then dig into it with salsa and crisp tortilla chips.

Aïoli

This garlic mayonnaise features in many traditional Provençal recipes, but also makes a delicious dip, surrounded by a selection of vegetables.

NUTRITIONAL INFORMATION

Calories 239	Sugars 0g
Protein 1g	Fat 26g
Carbohydrate 1g	Saturates 4g

15 mins   0 mins

SERVES 6

INGREDIENTS

about 4 large garlic cloves, or to taste

2 large egg yolks

1¼ cups extra-virgin olive oil

1–2 tbsp lemon juice

1 tbsp fresh white bread crumbs

sea salt and pepper

TO SERVE (OPTIONAL)

a selection of raw vegetables, such as sliced red bell peppers, zucchini slices, whole scallions, and tomato wedges

a selection of blanched and cooled vegetables, such as baby artichoke hearts, cauliflower or broccoli florets, or green beans

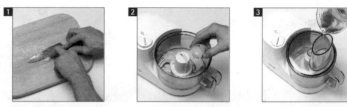

COOK'S TIP

The amount of garlic in a traditional Provençal aïoli is a matter of personal taste. Local cooks use 2 cloves per person as a rule of thumb, but this version is slightly milder, although still bursting with flavor.

1 Finely chop the garlic on a cutting board. Add a pinch of sea salt to the garlic and use the tip and broad side of a knife to work the garlic and salt into a smooth paste.

2 Transfer the garlic paste to a food processor. Add the egg yolks and process until well blended, scraping down the side of the bowl with a rubber spatula, if necessary.

3 With the motor running, slowly pour in the olive oil in a steady stream through the feeder tube, processing until a thick mayonnaise forms.

4 Add 1 tablespoon of the lemon juice and the bread crumbs and process again. Taste and add more lemon juice if necessary. Season to taste with sea salt and pepper.

5 Place the aïoli in a bowl, cover, and chill until ready to serve. To serve, place the bowl of aïoli on a large platter and surround with a selection of raw and lightly blanched vegetables.

Tapenade

These robust olive and anchovy spreads can be as thick or as thin as you like. They make flavorful appetizers spread on toast.

10–15 mins   5 mins

SERVES 6

I N G R E D I E N T S

thin slices of day-old baguette (optional)

olive oil (optional)

sprigs of fresh flatleaf parsley, to garnish

B L A C K   O L I V E   T A P E N A D E

2¼ cups black Niçoise olives in brine, rinsed
 and pitted

1 large garlic clove

2 tbsp walnut pieces

4 canned anchovy fillets, drained

about ½ cup extra-virgin olive oil

lemon juice, to taste

pepper

G R E E N   O L I V E   T A P E N A D E

2¼ cups green olives in brine, rinsed
 and pitted

4 canned anchovy fillets, rinsed

4 tbsp blanched almonds

1 tbsp capers in brine or vinegar, rinsed

about ½ cup extra-virgin olive oil

1½–3 tsp finely grated orange rind

pepper

1 To make the black olive tapenade, put the olives, garlic, walnut pieces, and anchovies in a food processor and process until blended.

2 With the motor running, slowly add the olive oil through the feeder tube, as if making mayonnaise. Add lemon juice and pepper to taste. Transfer to a bowl, cover with plastic wrap, and chill until required.

3 To make the green olive tapenade, put the olives, anchovies, almonds, and capers in a food processor and process until blended. With the motor running, slowly add the olive oil through the feeder tube, as if making mayonnaise. Add orange rind and pepper to taste. Transfer to a bowl, cover with plastic wrap, and chill until required.

4 To serve on croûtes, if desired, toast the slices of bread on both sides, until crisp. Brush 1 side of each slice with a little olive oil while they are still hot, so the oil is absorbed by the toast.

5 Spread the croûtes with the tapenade of your choice and garnish with parsley.

Chorizo & Garbanzo Tapas

A glass of chilled sherry and a selection of Spanish tapas is a great way to unwind at the end of the day.

NUTRITIONAL INFORMATION

Calories	462	Sugars	.........3g
Protein	........18g	Fat	..........36g
Carbohydrate	...17g	Saturates	.......9g

🍲 10 mins   🕐 8 mins

SERVES 4

INGREDIENTS

scant ½ cup olive oil

about 2 tbsp sherry vinegar

9 oz/250 g fresh chorizo sausage, in 1 piece

1 small Bermuda onion, finely chopped

14 oz/400 g canned garbanzo beans

salt and pepper

fresh oregano or flatleaf parsley, finely chopped, to garnish

chunks of fresh bread, to serve

1 Place 6 tablespoons of the olive oil and 2 tablespoons of vinegar in a bowl and whisk together. Taste and add a little more sherry vinegar, if desired. Season with salt and pepper to taste and set aside.

2 Using a small, sharp knife, remove the casing from the chorizo sausage. Cut the meat into ¼-inch/5-mm thick slices, then cut each slice into half-moon shapes.

3 Heat the remaining olive oil in a small, heavy skillet over medium-high heat. Add the onion and cook, stirring occasionally, for 2–3 minutes. Add the pieces of chorizo sausage and cook for about 3 minutes, or until the chorizo is cooked through.

4 Using a slotted spoon, remove the sausage and onion and drain on crumpled paper towels. Transfer to the bowl with the dressing and stir together.

5 Empty the garbanzo beans into a strainer and rinse well under cold running water; shake off the excess water. Add to the bowl with the other ingredients and stir together. Set aside to cool.

6 Just before serving, taste and adjust the seasoning. Spoon the salad into a serving bowl and sprinkle with chopped fresh oregano or parsley. Serve with chunks of fresh bread.

Red Shrimp Curry

Like all Thai curries, this one has as its base a paste
of chiles and other spices and a sauce of coconut milk.

NUTRITIONAL INFORMATION

Calories	149	Sugars	.........4g
Protein	........15g	Fat	...........7g
Carbohydrate	....6g	Saturates	.......1g

🥘 15 mins   ⏱ 10 mins

SERVES 4

I N G R E D I E N T S

2 tbsp vegetable oil

1 garlic clove, finely chopped

1 tbsp red curry paste (see below)

scant 1 cup coconut milk

2 tbsp Thai fish sauce

1 tsp sugar

12 large raw shrimp, deveined

2 kaffir lime leaves, finely shredded

1 small fresh red chile, seeded and
   thinly sliced

10 leaves Thai basil, if available, or
   ordinary basil

R E D   C U R R Y   P A S T E

3 dried long red chilies

½ tsp ground coriander

¼ tsp ground cumin

½ tsp ground black pepper

2 garlic cloves, chopped

2 lemongrass stalks, chopped

1 kaffir lime leaf, finely chopped

1 tsp grated fresh gingerroot or galangal

1 tsp shrimp paste (optional)

½ tsp salt

1 To make the red curry paste, put all the ingredients in
a blender or spice grinder and blend to a smooth paste,
adding a little water if necessary. Alternatively, pound the
ingredients together using a mortar and pestle, until
smooth. Set aside.

2 Heat the oil in a wok or skillet, until almost smoking.
Add the chopped garlic and cook until golden. Add
1 tablespoon of the curry paste and cook, stirring
constantly, for another minute. Add half the coconut milk
with the fish sauce and the sugar. Stir well, until the
mixture has thickened slightly.

3 Add the shrimp and simmer for 3–4 minutes, until they
turn color. Add the remaining coconut milk, the
lime leaves, and the fresh red chile. Cook for another
2–3 minutes, until the shrimp are just tender.

4 Add the basil leaves and stir until wilted. Transfer to a
warmed serving dish and serve immediately.

Fish with Black Bean Sauce

Steaming is one of the preferred methods of cooking whole fish in China because it maintains both the flavor and the texture.

NUTRITIONAL INFORMATION

Calories	292	Sugars	.........3g
Protein	........44g	Fat	...........7g
Carbohydrate	....6g	Saturates	....0.4g

🕙 10 mins   🕙 10 mins

SERVES 4

I N G R E D I E N T S

2 lb/900 g whole snapper, cleaned and scaled

3 garlic cloves, crushed

2 tbsp black bean sauce

1 tsp cornstarch

2 tsp sesame oil

2 tbsp light soy sauce

2 tsp superfine sugar

2 tbsp dry sherry

1 small leek, shredded

1 small red bell pepper, seeded and cut into thin strips

shredded leek and lemon wedges, to garnish

boiled rice or noodles, to serve

1 Rinse the fish inside and out with cold running water and pat dry with paper towels.

2 Make 2–3 diagonal slashes in the flesh on each side of the fish, using a sharp knife. Rub the garlic into the fish.

3 Combine the black bean sauce, cornstarch, sesame oil, light soy sauce, sugar, and dry sherry.

4 Place the fish in a shallow heatproof dish and pour the sauce mixture over the top. Sprinkle the shredded leek and bell pepper strips over the sauce.

5 Place the dish in the top of a steamer, cover, and steam for 10 minutes, or until the fish is cooked through.

6 Transfer the fish to a serving dish, garnish with shredded leek and lemon wedges, and serve immediately with boiled rice or noodles.

COOK'S TIP

Insert the point of a sharp knife into the fish to test if it is cooked. The fish is cooked through if the knife goes into the flesh easily.

Herrings with Hot Pesto

Oily fish, such as herrings and mackerel, form a vital part of the healthy diet because they are rich in essential omega 3 fatty acids.

NUTRITIONAL INFORMATION

Calories 382	Sugars 2g	
Protein 28g	Fat 29g	
Carbohydrate 3g	Saturates 5g	

10 mins   10 mins

SERVES 4

I N G R E D I E N T S

4 herrings or small mackerel, cleaned and gutted

2 tbsp olive oil

8 oz/225 g tomatoes, skinned, seeded, and chopped

8 canned anchovy fillets in oil, drained and chopped

about 30 fresh basil leaves

2 oz/55 g pine nuts

2 garlic cloves, crushed

1 Cook the herrings or mackerel under a preheated broiler for about 8–10 minutes on each side, or until the skin is slightly charred on both sides.

2 Meanwhile, heat 1 tablespoon of the olive oil in a large pan. Add the tomatoes and anchovies and cook over medium heat for 5 minutes.

3 To make the pesto sauce, put the basil, pine nuts, garlic, and remaining oil into a food processor and process to form a smooth paste. Alternatively, pound the ingredients by hand in a mortar with a pestle.

4 Add the pesto mixture to the pan of tomato and anchovies and stir to heat through.

5 Spoon some of the pesto sauce onto warmed individual serving plates. Place the fish on top and pour the rest of the pesto sauce over the fish. Serve immediately.

Mediterranean Monkfish

Some of the best seafood dishes are the simplest and this recipe proves the point. This is a delicious dish to serve in the summer.

NUTRITIONAL INFORMATION	
Calories 401	Sugars 5g
Protein 39g	Fat 25g
Carbohydrate 6g	Saturates 7g

🥘 15 mins   🕐 16–18 mins

SERVES 4

I N G R E D I E N T S

1 lb 5 oz/600 g cherry tomatoes, a mixture of yellow and red, if available

2 monkfish fillets, about 12 oz/350 g each

8 tbsp pesto sauce

salt and pepper

sprigs of fresh basil, to garnish

freshly cooked new potatoes, to serve

1 Cut the tomatoes in half and spread out, cut sides up, on the bottom of an ovenproof serving dish. Set aside.

2 Using your fingers, rub off the thin gray membrane that covers the monkfish.

3 If the skin has not been removed, place the fish skin side down on the counter. Loosen enough skin at one end of the fillet so you can grip it. Work from the

front to the back. Insert the knife, almost flat, and, using a gentle sawing action, remove the skin. Rinse the fillets well and pat dry with paper towels.

4 Place the fillets on top of the tomatoes, tucking the thin end under, if necessary (see Cook's Tip). Spread 4 tablespoons of the pesto sauce over each fillet and season with pepper.

5 Cover the dish tightly with foil, shiny side down. Place in a preheated oven, 450°F/230°C, and roast for 16–18 minutes, until the fish is cooked through, the flesh flakes easily, and the tomatoes are collapsing into a thick sauce.

6 Adjust the seasoning, if necessary. Garnish with basil sprigs and serve immediately with cooked new potatoes.

COOK'S TIP

Monkfish fillets are often cut from the tail, which means one end is much thinner than the rest and prone to overcooking. If you can't get fillets that are the same thickness, fold the thin end under to ensure even cooking.

Gingered Monkfish

This dish is a real treat and is perfect for special occasions. Monkfish has a tender flavor, which is ideal with asparagus, chili sauce, and ginger.

NUTRITIONAL INFORMATION

Calories	133	Sugars	.........0g
Protein	........21g	Fat	..........5g
Carbohydrate	....1g	Saturates	.......1g

5 mins ⏲ 10 mins

SERVES 4

I N G R E D I E N T S

1 lb/450 g monkfish

1 tbsp grated fresh gingerroot

2 tbsp sweet chili sauce

1 tbsp corn oil

3½ oz/100 g fine asparagus

3 scallions, sliced

1 tsp sesame oil

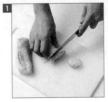 

1 Remove any membrane from the monkfish. Using a sharp knife, cut the monkfish into thin, flat, round slices. Set aside until required.

2 Combine the grated gingerroot and the sweet chili sauce in a small bowl, until thoroughly blended. Brush the ginger and chili sauce mixture over the monkfish pieces, using a pastry brush.

3 Heat the corn oil in a large preheated wok or heavy skillet.

4 Add the monkfish pieces, asparagus, and chopped scallions to the wok or skillet and cook over medium heat for about 5 minutes, constantly stirring very gently so the fish pieces do not break up.

5 Remove the wok or skillet from the heat, drizzle the sesame oil over the stir-fry, and toss gently to combine.

6 Transfer the stir-fried gingered monkfish to warm serving plates and serve immediately.

COOK'S TIP

Monkfish is quite expensive, but it is well worth using because it has a marvelous flavor and texture. Otherwise, you could use cubes of chunky cod fillet instead.

Spicy Tomato Chicken

These lowfat, spicy skewers are cooked in a matter of minutes—assemble them ahead of time and store in the refrigerator until you need them.

NUTRITIONAL INFORMATION

Calories 195	Sugars 11g
Protein 28g	Fat 4g
Carbohydrate ...12g	Saturates 1g

🍲 10 mins   ⏲ 10 mins

SERVES 4

INGREDIENTS

1 lb 2 oz/500 g skinless, boneless chicken breast

3 tbsp tomato paste

2 tbsp honey

2 tbsp Worcestershire sauce

1 tbsp chopped fresh rosemary

9 oz/250 g cherry tomatoes

sprigs of fresh rosemary, to garnish

couscous or rice, to serve

COOK'S TIP

Couscous is made from semolina that has been made into separate grains. It usually just needs moistening or steaming before serving.

1 Cut the chicken into 1-inch/2.5-cm chunks and place in a bowl.

2 Combine the tomato paste, honey, Worcestershire sauce, and chopped rosemary in a small bowl. Add to the chicken, stirring to coat evenly.

3 Alternating the chicken pieces and cherry tomatoes, thread them onto

8 wooden skewers. (If the skewers have been soaked in water they will not char.)

4 Spoon over any remaining glaze. Cook under a preheated hot broiler for about 8–10 minutes, turning occasionally, until the chicken is thoroughly cooked.

5 Serve on a bed of couscous or rice and garnish with sprigs of rosemary.

Chicken & Corn Stir-Fry

This quick and healthy dish is stir-fried, which means you need use only the minimum of oil for cooking.

NUTRITIONAL INFORMATION

Calories	280	Sugars	........7g
Protein	.......31g	Fat	..........11g
Carbohydrate	....9g	Saturates	.......2g

5 mins   10 mins

SERVES 4

INGREDIENTS

4 skinless, boneless chicken breasts

9 oz/250 g baby corn cobs

9 oz/250 g snow peas

2 tbsp sunflower oil

1 tbsp sherry vinegar

1 tbsp honey

1 tbsp light soy sauce

1 tbsp sunflower seeds

pepper

rice or Chinese egg noodles, to serve

1 Using a sharp knife, slice the chicken into long, thin strips.

2 Cut the baby corn cobs in half lengthwise and trim the snow peas.

3 Heat the sunflower oil in a preheated wok or a wide skillet.

4 Add the chicken and stir-fry over fairly high heat for 1 minute.

5 Add the baby corn cobs and snow peas and stir-fry over moderate heat for 5–8 minutes, until evenly cooked. The vegetables should be tender but still slightly crunchy.

6 Combine the sherry vinegar, honey, and soy sauce in a small bowl.

7 Stir the vinegar mixture into the wok or skillet with the sunflower seeds.

8 Season to taste with pepper. Cook, stirring constantly, for 1 minute.

9 Serve the chicken and corn stir-fry hot with rice or Chinese egg noodles.

VARIATION

Rice vinegar or balsamic vinegar make good substitutes for the sherry vinegar.

Skewered Chicken Spirals

These unusual chicken kabobs have a marvelous Italian flavor, and the bacon helps keep them moist during cooking.

NUTRITIONAL INFORMATION

Calories 231   Sugars 1g
Protein . . . . .29g   Fat 13g
Carbohydrate . . . .1g   Saturates 5g

15 mins   10 mins

SERVES 4

INGREDIENTS

4 skinless, boneless chicken breasts

1 garlic clove, crushed

2 tbsp tomato paste

4 slices smoked lean bacon

large handful of fresh basil leaves

vegetable oil, for brushing

salt and pepper

salad greens, to serve

1 Spread out a piece of chicken between two sheets of plastic wrap and beat firmly with a rolling pin or meat mallet to flatten the chicken to an even thickness. Repeat with the remaining chicken breasts.

2 Combine the garlic and tomato paste and spread the mixture over the chicken. Lay a bacon slice over each, then sprinkle with the basil. Season with salt and pepper to taste.

3 Roll up each piece of chicken firmly, then cut into thick slices. Thread the slices onto 4 skewers, making sure the skewers hold the chicken in spiral shapes.

4 Brush lightly with oil and then cook on a hot barbecue grill or under a preheated broiler for about 10 minutes, turning once. Serve hot with salad greens.

Pork Stir-Fry with Vegetables

This is a very simple dish, which lends itself to almost any combination of vegetables that you have at hand.

NUTRITIONAL INFORMATION

Calories 216   Sugars 3g
Protein . . . . .19g   Fat 12g
Carbohydrate . . . .5g   Saturates 3g

5 mins   15 mins

SERVES 4

I N G R E D I E N T S

2 tbsp vegetable oil

2 garlic cloves, crushed

½-inch/1-cm piece of fresh gingerroot, cut into slivers

12 oz/350 g lean pork tenderloin, thinly sliced

1 carrot, cut into thin strips

1 red bell pepper, seeded and diced

1 fennel bulb, sliced

1 oz/25 g water chestnuts, halved

1½ cups bean sprouts

2 tbsp Chinese rice wine

1¼ cups pork bouillon or chicken bouillon

pinch of dark brown sugar

1 tsp cornstarch

2 tsp water

1 Heat the oil in a preheated wok. Add the garlic, ginger, and pork. Stir-fry for 1–2 minutes, until the meat is seared.

2 Add the carrot, bell pepper, fennel, and water chestnuts and stir-fry for about 2-3 minutes.

3 Add the bean sprouts and stir-fry for 1 minute. Remove the pork and vegetables, set aside, and keep warm.

4 Add the Chinese rice wine, pork bouillon or chicken bouillon, and the sugar to the wok. Blend the cornstarch to a smooth paste with the water and stir it into the sauce. Bring to a boil, stirring constantly, until thickened and clear.

5 Return the meat and vegetables to the wok and cook for 1–2 minutes, until heated through and coated with the sauce. Serve immediately.

VARIATION
Use dry sherry instead of the Chinese rice wine if you have difficulty obtaining it.

Stir-Fried Pork with Pasta

This delicious dish, with its hint of Thai flavors, will certainly get the taste buds tingling—and it's ready in next to no time.

NUTRITIONAL INFORMATION

Calories 751	Sugars 10g
Protein 37g	Fat 27g
Carbohydrate . . .96g	Saturates 8g

🗋 🗋

🍲 10 mins   🕐 15 mins

SERVES 4

I N G R E D I E N T S

3 tbsp sesame oil

12 oz/350 g pork tenderloin, cut into thin strips

1 lb/450 g dried taglioni

8 shallots, sliced

2 garlic cloves, finely chopped

1-inch/2.5-cm piece of fresh gingerroot, grated

1 fresh green chile, finely chopped

1 red bell pepper, seeded and thinly sliced

1 green bell pepper, seeded and thinly sliced

3 zucchini, thinly sliced

2 tbsp ground almonds

1 tsp ground cinnamon

1 tbsp oyster sauce

2 oz/55 g creamed coconut, grated

salt and pepper

COOK'S TIP

Creamed coconut is available from Chinese and Asian food stores and some large supermarkets. It is sold in the form of compressed blocks and adds a concentrated coconut flavor to the dish.

1 Heat the sesame oil in a preheated wok. Season the pork with salt and pepper to taste, add to the wok, and stir-fry for 5 minutes.

2 Meanwhile, bring a large pan of lightly salted water to a boil. Add the taglioni, bring back to a boil, and cook for about 10 minutes, until just tender but still firm to the bite. Drain, set the pasta aside, and keep warm.

3 Add the shallots, garlic, ginger, and chile to the wok and stir-fry for 2 minutes. Add the bell peppers and zucchini and stir-fry for 1 minute.

4 Finally, add the ground almonds, cinnamon, oyster sauce, and creamed coconut to the wok and stir-fry for about 1 minute.

5 Transfer the taglioni to a warmed serving dish. Top with the stir-fry and serve immediately.

Pork Balls with Mint Sauce

Made with lean ground pork, the balls are first stir-fried, then braised in the wok with bouillon and pickled walnuts to give a tangy flavor.

NUTRITIONAL INFORMATION

Calories 318	Sugars 2g	
Protein 30g	Fat 20g	
Carbohydrate 6g	Saturates 5g	

5 mins   25 mins

SERVES 4

I N G R E D I E N T S

1 lb 2 oz/500 g lean ground pork

¾ cup fine fresh white bread crumbs

½ tsp ground allspice

1 garlic clove, crushed

2 tbsp chopped fresh mint

1 egg, beaten

2 tbsp sunflower oil

1 red bell pepper, seeded

generous 1 cup chicken bouillon

4 pickled walnuts, sliced

salt and pepper

sprigs of fresh mint, to garnish

rice or Chinese noodles, to serve

1 Combine the ground pork, bread crumbs, allspice, garlic, and half the chopped mint in a mixing bowl. Season to taste with salt and pepper, then bind together with the beaten egg.

2 Shape the meat mixture into 20 small balls with your hands, dampening your hands if it is easier for shaping.

3 Heat the sunflower oil in a wok or heavy skillet, swirling the oil around until really hot, then add the pork balls and stir-fry for about 4–5 minutes, or until browned all over.

4 Use a slotted spoon to remove the pork balls from the wok as they are cooked, then drain thoroughly on absorbent paper towels.

5 Pour off all but 1 tablespoon of fat and oil from the wok or skillet. Thinly slice the red bell pepper, then add to the pan and stir-fry for 2–3 minutes, or until the slices begin to soften but not color.

6 Add the chicken bouillon and bring to a boil. Season well with salt and pepper and return the pork balls to the wok, stirring well to coat in the sauce.

Simmer for 7–10 minutes, turning the pork balls from time to time.

7 Add the remaining chopped mint and the pickled walnuts to the wok and continue to simmer for 2–3 minutes, turning the pork balls regularly to coat them in the sauce.

8 Adjust the seasoning and serve the pork balls with rice or Chinese noodles or with a stir-fried vegetable dish, garnished with sprigs of fresh mint.

Vegetable Frittata

A frittata is a type of Italian omelet—you can add almost anything to the eggs. It is also delicious eaten cold and makes an ideal picnic dish.

NUTRITIONAL INFORMATION

Calories	...310	Sugars	...4g
Protein	...18g	Fat	...17g
Carbohydrate	...24g	Saturates	...4g

🥔 15 mins   ⏱ 20 mins

SERVES 4

INGREDIENTS

3 tbsp olive oil

1 onion, chopped

2 garlic cloves, chopped

8 oz/225 g zucchini, thinly sliced

4 eggs

14 oz/400 g canned borlotti beans, rinsed and drained

3 tomatoes, skinned and chopped

2 tbsp chopped fresh parsley

1 tbsp chopped fresh basil

½ cup grated Swiss cheese

salt and pepper

1 Heat 2 tablespoons of the oil in a skillet. Add the onion and garlic and cook over medium heat, stirring occasionally, for 2–3 minutes, or until softened. Add the zucchini and cook, stirring occasionally, for 3–4 minutes, or until softened.

2 Break the eggs into a bowl and season with salt and pepper to taste. Beat lightly and stir in the onion and zucchini mixture with the beans, tomatoes, parsley, and basil.

3 Heat the remaining oil in a 9½-inch/ 24-cm omelet pan with a heatproof handle, add the egg mixture, and cook over low heat for approximately 5 minutes, until the eggs have almost set and the underside of the frittata is golden brown.

4 Sprinkle the cheese over the top and place the pan under a preheated moderate broiler for 3–4 minutes, or until set on the top but still moist in the middle. Cut into wedges and serve warm or at room temperature.

COOK'S TIP

Swiss cheese is made from unpasteurized cow's milk and has a sweet, nutty flavor, which enhances the taste of this frittata. It is firm and close textured, and has small holes interspersed throughout.